Welcome to SAVANNAH

— Garry Patrick
General Manager

my HOMETOWN

WELCOME ABOARD!

We are pleased that you have chosen Old Town Trolley Tours to guide you on your trip through the Historic District of Savannah. Our expert tour conductors will entertain and inform as they navigate the trolleys past some of the most significant points of interest to include historic homes and museums, beautiful squares and parks, River Street, magnificent monuments and modern day attractions such as Paula Deen's The Lady & Sons Restaurant. Along the way, the trolley will stop at 15 well placed stops which are located throughout the Historic District. This guidebook has been designed around these 15 stops as a supplement to the trolley tour.

The walking tours connected with each stop are "loop" tours of varying lengths which begin at the designated numbered stop and end at the same stop. We always encourage you to board the trolley at the same stop that you departed so that you do not miss any of the tour content. The walking tours include additional sites and points of interest that you can explore on foot.

The stop index and map at the back of the book allow you to quickly determine which stops are near which points of interest. In terms of navigation during the walking tours, just remember that the river is always to your north. If you ever get disoriented, just ask anyone "Which way to River Street?" and that direction will be north.

Savannah is not just a place. It's a unique and fragile treasure. A place that matters. And its visitors are not just numbers. They are discriminating heritage travelers who expect (and deserve) quality and authenticity. Historic Savannah Foundation and Old Town Trolley Tours work together to protect, preserve and promote this city so folks like you can more fully experience these gifts of history, architecture and charm.

This guide is an 'appetizer' to enjoying all that Savannah has to offer—from General Oglethorpe's original city plan to an overlay of 18th, 19th and 20th century buildings and from outstanding restaurants to an array of museums. Let this publication whet your appetite for a deeper exploration of Savannah. In so doing, you will find places that matter to you…and you will be inspired to do something about protecting and preserving them. We all share responsibility for stewarding this city; you can do your part by respecting its delicate balance.

Historic Savannah Foundation (HSF) is the recognized leader of the local preservation movement. For nearly 60 years, HSF has endeavored to preserve the Savannah you came to enjoy. Through advocacy and educational programs, HSF protects the irreplaceable. And, remarkably, we use our own resources to acquire, stabilize and sell endangered historic properties to preservation-minded buyers through our nationally recognized Revolving Fund. We have saved more than 300 historic buildings in the Landmark District alone, and we're not finished yet! Why? Because the Landmark District is but one of 13 historic districts in and around Savannah where history is being made every day. We encourage you to learn more about the 'other' parts of Savannah that are equally compelling. If we don't preserve and appreciate our shared heritage, how will we know who we are as a people?

That's why you are so important to us. By taking a tour and familiarizing yourself with our history and architecture, you become sensitized to its importance. And you become a more responsible visitor…a temporary steward, if you will. So take in all you can. And then take home a deeper appreciation for this city and the preservation movement. Know that your support of Historic Savannah Foundation and Old Town Trolley Tours helps bring much needed resources to the on-going protection of one of America's most beautiful and historic cities.

Daniel G. Carey
President & CEO

 This mark identifies historic points of interest that Historic Savannah Foundation has protected and preserved for future generations to enjoy.
www.myHSF.org

Savannah's History
A Brief Overview

On November 17, 1732 a 36-year-old James Edward Oglethorpe and 113 other colonists departed England bound for America. Their mission was to establish the colony of Georgia, named in honor of King George II who had granted its Charter. The new colony was intended to provide an additional source of natural resources for England as well as to serve as a military buffer zone between the Spanish pushing northward from Florida and the already established English colony of South Carolina. The Charter for the new colony prohibited slavery, lawyers, Catholics and hard liquor. Over time all of these prohibitions were eliminated.

The colonists' ship, the *Ann*, made landfall on January 13, 1733 near Charleston, SC. From there, the colonists sailed south to an area around Port Royal, SC where they waited for Oglethorpe to go ahead with a small group to scout out the site of the new colony. He chose the location of what is now Downtown Savannah for several reasons. It was high ground which could be easily defended and the river bluff allowed large ships to draft close to the bank. The river also provided a source of fresh water. In addition, the Yamacraw Indians, being familiar with the land, had chosen it as the site of their village. Fortunately, the Indians, led by Tomochichi, were friendly and open to the colonists settling on the bluff. Oglethorpe returned to get the colonists and the entire group arrived on the bluff on February 12, 1733.

With the help of William Bull, a civil engineer from Charleston, Oglethorpe proceeded to lay out the new town. No one knows for sure where or how Oglethorpe came up with the plan for Savannah, but there is little doubt that his design directly influenced the unique environment that has grown up around it. The basic component of his plan was a ward. It was comprised of 8 blocks. The larger four blocks are called tything blocks which are further subdivided by east-west lanes. The four smaller blocks that front the squares are known as trust lots. The plan intended the tything blocks to be used for residential purposes while the trust lots would serve as the sites of civic and commercial structures. The city could be expanded by simply replicating the pattern.

STATUE OF GENERAL OGLETHORPE IN CHIPPEWA SQUARE

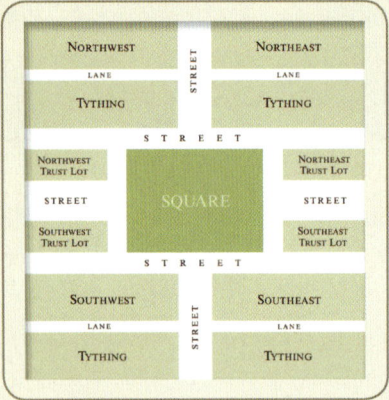

TYPICAL WARD

The original plan called for 4 squares (now known as Johnson, Wright, Ellis and Telfair). By 1851, the city had grown to include 24 squares. Today 22 squares remain including Ellis, which reopened in 2010.

During the Revolutionary War, the British took control of Savannah in 1778. In 1779, a large French and American force attempted to take the city by siege and later by direct assault (The Siege of Savannah) but they failed. The British retained control of Savannah until the Americans ultimately won the war.

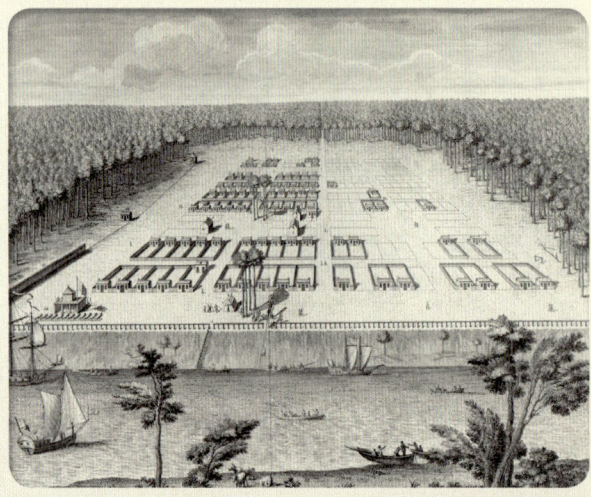

VIEW OF SAVANNAH IN 1734

With American Independence secured, Savannah and its economy blossomed. The soil and climate were found to be particularly favorable for the production of rice and cotton. However, picking out lint and cotton seeds manually was a labor intensive process which limited cotton's viability as a revenue generator. In 1793, Eli Whitney invented the cotton gin which mechanically separated the seeds from cotton. His invention allowed land and plantation owners to make huge profits growing cotton for export to England. The port of Savannah and the shipping merchants also benefited from

A BIRD'S-EYE VIEW NORTH FROM WRIGHT SQUARE IN 1909.

this economic boom. It was during this antebellum period that many of the great mansions, public buildings and churches of Savannah were constructed. Massive fires in 1796 and 1820 each wiped out half of the town and a yellow fever outbreak in 1820 killed a tenth of the population but Savannah was resilient. It became known as one of the most picturesque cities in America populated by a unique and cultured citizenry. Then, the Civil War began.

In 1862, Fort Pulaski was captured by Union forces and held through the remainder of the war. Possession of the fort allowed the Union to impose a sea blockade that crippled the city and its economy. Union General, William T. Sherman, took Savannah with little effort on December 21, 1864. His forces had burned and destroyed everything they encountered on their March to the Sea from Atlanta but Sherman was awed by Savannah's beauty and chose not to destroy it. Instead he presented it to President Lincoln as a Christmas gift.

PULASKI MONUMENT

NAVAL STORES (C1885)

CONFEDERATE MONUMENT

After the war, reconstruction efforts began. It was a slow process but by the turn of the century Savannah's economy was strong again. Cotton led the way and Savannah also became a leader in exporting lumber and naval stores (products such as resin related to the construction and maintenance of wooden ships). Economic troubles would visit Savannah again in the early 1900s in the form of the boll weevil, which ravaged cotton production in the Southeast, and the advent of metal ships. Savannah would not right itself again until the 1950's when a broader based economy took hold.

It was also during this time that a group of civic-minded women formed Historic Savannah Foundation, which is credited with beginning the movement to save Savannah's historic structures. They had been spurred to action by witnessing the loss of several of the city's architectural treasures. In 1966, the Savannah Historic District was declared a National Historic Landmark. Fortunately, the great significance of Savannah's past was recognized and protected early enough to preserve its charm for future generations.

SAVANNAH VISITORS CENTER & HISTORY MUSEUM

TROLLEY STOP

THIS BUILDING PREVIOUSLY SERVED AS THE PASSENGER TERMINAL FOR THE CENTRAL RAILROAD and Banking Company of Georgia (later Central of Georgia Railway). The last passenger train departed from here in 1971. The Railroad also operated buildings to the north and south of this terminal. Any visitor to Savannah should stop here. Friendly greeters will provide information about all things of interest in Savannah. In addition, there are gift shops and theatres showing history films of Savannah. The Museum contains many items of interest including a classic Central of Georgia Locomotive, a working cotton gin, a replica of the "Bird Girl" statue and the actual bench used in the movie Forrest Gump.

WALK NORTH ON MARTIN LUTHER KING JR. BLVD.

 THE RED BUILDING - EICHBERG HALL (c1887) This building originally served as a terminal and administrative offices for the Central of Georgia Railway. SCAD saved this building from demolition in 1988 when it purchased and renovated the building and terminal sheds to serve as the architecture, historic preservation, interior design and urban design departments of the school.

 THE GRAY BUILDING - KIAH HALL- SCAD MUSEUM OF ART (c1856) This Greek Revival style building is the oldest surviving railroad office building in the United States. A Savannah Daily News story in 1859 called it "a marvel of solidity and beauty." It predates the Red Building and the passenger terminal where the Savannah Visitor Center is located. It served as the headquarters of the Central of Georgia Railway. The Savannah College of Art and Design (SCAD) renamed the building Kiah Hall in honor of African-American artist Virginia Jackson Kiah. Today it houses the SCAD Museum of Art (open to the public) and the Earle W. Newton Center for British and American Studies.

TURN AROUND AND WALK BACK SOUTH ON MLK, JR. BLVD.

 OLD TOWN TROLLEY - SEGWAY TOURS - GRIBBLE HOUSE PARANORMAL EXPERIENCE- Located just across MLK from the , this is a great location for purchasing discounted tickets to many of the attractions that you will want to see while you are here in Savannah. This building is also home to Segway of Savannah. If you've ever wanted to ride on a Segway, now is your chance. Various Segway tours and adventures depart from here.

The Eliza Gribble House was formerly located on this site. On December 10, 1909, three women were murdered in this house and the crime drew international attention. The Gribble House Paranormal Experience is an attraction located in this building. Each night, you can participate with professional ghost hunters on a two hour ghost hunting experience using the latest, state-of-the art equipment.

(Discounted tickets for both of these attractions are available thru Old Town Trolley.)

 **CONTINUE WALKING SOUTH ON MLK, JR. CROSSING OVER LIBERTY ST./LOUISVILLE RD.**

1d BATTLEFIELD MEMORIAL PARK - This memorial is a replica of the Spring Hill Redoubt that was the center of fighting during the Revolutionary War's "Siege of Savannah." The actual location of this redoubt is a little further west of this location but the battle occurred all around this area. In the early morning hours of October 9, 1779, a combined French and American force of approximately 5,500 troops launched a disorganized attack to take back Savannah from the British. The British force of about 2,500 troops was entrenched and prepared to defend the city. It is believed that the British had advance knowledge of where the Franco-Americans intended to attack. In about one hour the second bloodiest battle of the Revolutionary War was over and the British were the decisive victors. The Franco Americans lost between 600 -1,000 men and the British lost only 18. William Jasper ③c and Casimir Pulaski ③h were among those patriots who fought and died here.

FIGHTING AT THE SPRING HILL REDOUBT, OCTOBER 9, 1779 ▶

1e ROUNDHOUSE RAILROAD MUSEUM - A favorite for kids of all ages, this museum features a large collection of historic locomotives and rolling stock. This massive facility, constructed in 1835, served as a train construction and repair facility for the Central of Georgia Railway. It is a part of the most complete antebellum railroad complex in the United States. Today you can ride on a train and take a spin on the large turntable.

THIS PHOTO FROM AROUND 1950 SHOWS THE ENTIRE CENTRAL OF GEORGIA RAILWAY COMPLEX. ▼

 TURN AROUND AND WALK BACK NORTH ON MARTIN LUTHER KING JR. BLVD. TO THE INTERSECTION OF MLK AND LIBERTY STREET/LOUISVILLE ROAD. USE THE CROSSWALK TO CROSS MLK AND WALK SOUTH ALONG MLK, JR.

1f MARRIOTT COURTYARD HOTEL - This hotel and the surrounding property was formerly the home of St. Patrick's Catholic Church.

◀ **ST. PATRICK'S CATHOLIC CHURCH -** Established as the second Catholic parish in Savannah after St. John's, this parish was organized in 1865 and the large Romanesque church was completed in 1879. During its time, West Broad Street (now Martin Luther King Jr. Blvd.) at Liberty Street was a significant commercial intersection. So prized was its real estate that the church was torn down in 1941 to make way for commercial development.

8

UNION STATION - The ornate Union Station was completed in 1902 at a cost of $150,000. This station and the surrounding areas were once the center of the African American community in Savannah. The station and much of the surrounding area was bulldozed in 1963 to make way for I-16.

1g INTERSTATE 16 - I-16 and this gas service station now occupy the former location of Union Station.

▶ This photo from 1919 of MLK Blvd. near Union Station shows the commercial vibrancy of this corridor. Unfortunately, the construction of I-16 bisected the neighborhood which led to a general decline of business activity in this area.

1h RALPH MARK GILBERT CIVIL RIGHTS MUSEUM - Opened in 1996, this museum is named for the father of Savannah's Civil Rights struggle, Rev. Ralph Mark Gilbert. Unique interactive exhibits, thought provoking videos and recreated Civil Rights settings give visitors an up-close history of African Americans in Savannah, from the early days of slavery through the struggle for Civil Rights.

 WALK NORTH ON MLK, JR. BLVD. AND RETURN TO STOP 1

BULL STREET CORRIDOR

TROLLEY STOP **2**

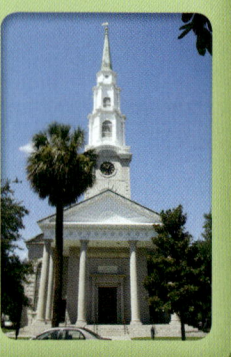

BULL STREET is the main north/south road in the Historic District and it divides east and west. It is named after Col. William Bull, a trained surveyor and one of the most prominent men in South Carolina at the time. Bull was appointed by the Governor of South Carolina to assist James Oglethorpe with establishing the new colony in Georgia.

INDEPENDENT PRESBYTERIAN CHURCH - Presbyterianism was introduced to the colony by Scottish Highlanders who were recruited to defend Savannah against Spanish Florida. This congregation was formed in 1755. The current structure was built in 1889-1890 and is a replica of the previous structure that burned in the fire of 1889. It is a white granite building of late Georgian colonial design. The interior is notable for its unusually high pulpit and the classic ornamentation of the vaulted ceiling. The massive steeple of this finely proportioned building is easily recognizable when viewing the skyline of Savannah.

 WALK NORTH ON BULL STREET. CROSS OVER OGLETHORPE AVE. TO **2a** AND CONTINUE TOWARD WRIGHT SQUARE.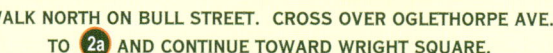

2a **JULIETTE GORDON LOW BIRTHPLACE -** This home was built originally for James Moore Wayne. Wayne served as the Mayor of Savannah from 1817-1819, a US Representative from Georgia from 1829-1835 and a US Supreme Court Justice for 32 years. Wayne sold the home to William Washington Gordon (see) in 1831. Gordon's granddaughter, Juliette Gordon Low, the founder of the Girl Scouts of America, was born in this house in 1860. The Girl Scouts purchased the home in 1953 and it now serves as a museum. It was designated as Savannah's First National Historic Landmark in 1965. At the time she founded the Girl Scouts, Mrs. Low was living in the Andrew Low House (see **6a** **6b** **6c**).

 WALK NORTH ON BULL STREET TO WRIGHT SQUARE.

WRIGHT SQUARE - One of the first four squares, this square was laid out in 1733. It was originally named Upper Square and was also known as Percival Square. This square served as the public market until the colonial legislature relocated it to Ellis Square in 1763. In that same year the square was renamed in honor of the last Royal Governor of Georgia, Sir James Wright.

2b **GORDON MONUMENT - (ERECTED 1883)**
This monument was placed in honor of William Washington Gordon. Gordon was one of Savannah's early mayors and he was instrumental in the expansion of the railroad system from Savannah to the interior areas of Georgia. He was the founder of the Central Railroad and Banking Company of Georgia. This monument took the place of Tomochichi's burial mound and it is believed his grave is still located underneath.

This photo from the 1850's shows Tomochichi's burial mound in its original location at the center of Wright Square.

2c **TOMOCHICHI'S ROCK -** This stone was placed in 1899 in honor of the Yamacraw Indian chief Tomochichi. His tribe occupied the bluff where Oglethorpe and the colonists landed but he agreed to relocate further upriver. The Indians and his colonists coexisted in peace primarily due to the leadership of Tomochichi. He died on October 5, 1739 and had requested to be buried among the colonists. He was

given a state funeral and Oglethorpe himself served as a pallbearer. When the Gordon Monument was placed over Tomochichi's grave, Nellie Kinzie Gordon (Gordon's daughter in law and mother of Juliette Gordon Low) headed a group that obtained the large granite stone from a quarry in Stone Mountain, GA.

This portrait of Tomochichi and his nephew Toonahowi was painted in England when they visited as guests of Oglethorpe.

2d **OLD CHATHAM COUNTY COURTHOUSE -** This building was constructed in 1889. At the time of its completion it was considered to be one of the finest public buildings in the entire southeast. This building is still used by the county but most of the court functions were relocated in 1979 to the current Chatham County Courthouse on Montgomery Street.

This photo shows the previous Chatham County Courthouse building that was constructed on the same site in 1833. During its time, its Greek Revival style matched the former Lutheran Church of the Ascension. (See **2e**).

10

2e LUTHERAN CHURCH OF THE ASCENSION - This congregation was organized in 1744 and the church originally constructed a wood frame structure on this site in 1756. The current gothic building was constructed between 1875 and 1879. The Lutheran Church in Savannah was founded by refugees from Salzburg, Bavaria who came to Georgia because of the colony's tolerance for persecuted Protestants. The stained glass windows in the sanctuary of this church are a spectacular sight.

The previous Lutheran church building on this site was built in 1843 in the Greek Revival style but it was mostly demolished to make way for the current gothic structure. ▲

2f US COURTHOUSE - Originally built in 1898 as a US Post Office, this building now occupies the Northwestern and Southwestern trust lots (including what used to be President Street). It is built of Georgia marble and it originally occupied only the Southwestern trust lot and was oriented perpendicular to Wright Square.

CHATHAM ARTILLERY ARMORY (c1849) - ▶ Originally occupying the northwestern trust lot on Wright Square, the Chatham Artillery Armory was the headquarters for the Chatham Artillery, a militia unit organized during the Revolutionary War. This unique building was demolished in 1930 to make way for the expansion of the US Courthouse.

▲ This photo shows the original footprint and orientation of the US Courthouse building toward President Street. Take a look at the panoramic photo at the top of page 6.

 WALK SOUTH ON BULL STREET. CROSS OVER OGLETHORPE AVE. AND CONTINUE TOWARD CHIPPEWA SQUARE.

CHIPPEWA SQUARE - Laid out in 1813, this square was named for the Battle of Chippawa where American forces had a decisive victory against the British in the War of 1812. The city misspelled the name of the square.

2g LOCATION OF FORREST GUMP'S BENCH- The bench where Forrest Gump (Tom Hanks) told his life story was located to the north end of this square fronting on Hull Street in-between the two crosswalks. The original bench is now located in the Savannah History Museum.

2h OGLETHORPE MONUMENT - (ERECTED 1910) This bronze statue of Oglethorpe is one of Savannah's most notable monuments. The statue was designed by Daniel Chester French who is also credited with Lincoln's statue in the Lincoln Memorial in Washington, D.C. In the tradition of orienting statues of military leaders towards their enemy, General Oglethorpe is facing south to keep a watchful eye on the Spanish in Florida.

11

2i **FIRST BAPTIST CHURCH (c1833) -** This congregation organized in 1800 and moved into this classic Greek Revival architecture building when it was completed in 1833. This church is the oldest original (never burned or reconstructed) church building in Savannah.

2j **PHILBRICK-EASTMAN HOUSE (COMPLETED 1847)** Now housing the headquarters of a local business, this fine building served as a residence for many distinguished Savannah families. It is best known for its iron fencing featuring profiles of famous poets and statesman. This ironwork is not original to this house. It is a remnant of a lost architectural treasure, the Barclay-Wetter House.

2k **SAVANNAH THEATRE - (OPENED 1818)** Originally designed by William Jay, this theatre is considered the oldest operating theatre in the United States. Very little of the original structure exists due to multiple fires and face-lifts. It was redesigned and rebuilt into its current Art Deco style as a result of a fire in 1948.

▲ *The chance to see a show put on by the talented actors of this theatre should not be missed.*

WALK NORTH ON BULL STREET BACK TO STOP 2.

MADISON SQUARE

TROLLEY STOP 3

MADISON SQUARE - LAID OUT IN 1837, this square was named in honor of James Madison, the fourth President of the United States.

MADISON SQUARE SOMETIME PRIOR TO 1925. ▶

3a **THE OLD SORREL-WEED HOUSE (c1841) -** Considered one of the finest examples of Greek Revival-Regency architecture in Savannah, this home was originally built for Francis Sorrel, a shipping merchant. It was sold to Henry Weed in 1859. This home was a social hotspot during the 1840's-50's and many prominent people were entertained here including General Robert E. Lee.

3b **THE DESOTO** - This site was previously occupied by the Hotel Desoto which opened in 1890. During its time it was a grand hotel that rivaled the finest hotels in New York and Florida. It was a Romanesque style building designed by William Gibbons Preston who also designed the Cotton Exchange (See **12b**), the Old Chatham County Courthouse (See **2d**) and the Savannah Volunteer Guards Armory (See **3g**). The original hotel building was torn down in 1966 and was replaced by the current more modern structure.

▲ HISTORIC HOTEL DESOTO

▲ "FIREPROOF, AND IT'S FAMOUS" A CATCHY SLOGAN IN 1931.

3c **SERGEANT JASPER MONUMENT** - This bronze statue honoring William Jasper was completed in 1888. Jasper was a Revolutionary hero from South Carolina who first earned distinction at the Battle of Sullivan's Island in Charleston. Ignoring heavy fire from the British fleet, he re-raised the American battle flag that had been shot down. This rallied the Americans to continue fighting and the British were defeated. During the Siege of Savannah in 1779, Jasper again tried to rally his fellow soldiers by raising their flag under heavy fire but this time he was shot and killed.

▲ JASPER RAISING THE FLAG AT THE SPRING HILL REDOUBT DURING THE SIEGE OF SAVANNAH.

3d **GREEN-MELDRIM HOUSE (c1853)** - This Gothic Revival home was originally built for Charles Green, an Englishman who was a wealthy cotton merchant. When Savannah was surrendered to the Union Army in December 1864, Green offered his home to General Sherman to serve as his headquarters while in Savannah. It was from here that Sherman sent his famous telegram to President Lincoln presenting the city as a Christmas gift. The home was later occupied by the Meldrim family who sold the home in 1943 to St. John's Episcopal Church to be used as a parish house.

THE MAN THAT SPARED SAVANNAH, ▶ MAJOR GENERAL WILLIAM TECUMSEH SHERMAN (c MAY 1865).

3e **ST. JOHN'S CHURCH** - Chartered as an expansion parish to Christ Church (See **11e**) in 1841, this building was built in 1853 and is known for its beautiful sounding bell chimes.

3f **GRYPHON TEA ROOM** - This unusual building was built as the Scottish Rite Temple in 1912. SCAD leases and operates the Gryphon Tea Room. The Scottish Rite's boys still use the building for meetings. The ground floor was once occupied by Solomon's Drug Store, one of the oldest pharmacies in the country.

3g **SCAD - POETTER HALL (c1893)** Originally constructed as the Savannah Volunteer Guards Armory, this is the first building that was purchased and renovated by the Savannah College of Art and Design or "SCAD." The school opened in this building in 1979. It is now known as Poetter Hall in honor of May and Paul Poetter who co-founded SCAD with Paula Wallace, the current president of the school, and Richard Rowan. SCAD has contributed greatly to the preservation of historic Savannah and now occupies over 60 buildings in the area.

 WALK SOUTH ON BULL STREET TO MONTEREY SQUARE.

MONTEREY SQUARE - Commemorating the Battle of Monterey where American forces captured the Mexican city of Monterey during the Mexican-American War, this square was laid out in 1847. It is considered by many Savannahians to be the most luxurious square in town.

3h **PULASKI MONUMENT (c1852)** Casimir Pulaski was a skilled Polish soldier who is known as "the father of American cavalry." He was exiled from Poland after rebelling against Russian rule. Benjamin Franklin recommended that General George Washington accept Pulaski as a volunteer. In a letter to Washington penned shortly after arriving in America, Pulaski wrote "I came here, where freedom is being defended, to serve it, and to live or die for it. Pulaski's cavalry charge at the Battle of Brandywine is credited with saving Washington's life. Pulaski died as a result of infection from a grapeshot wound suffered during the Siege of Savannah in 1779. The actual grapeshot extracted from Pulaski's thigh is on display at the Georgia Historical Society (see **4f**).

◀ It is believed that the remains interred underneath this monument are Pulaski's. In 1852 and 1996 respectively, groups of doctors determined that the remains are consistent with the known features of Pulaski. The group from 1996 hoped to prove his identity by DNA evidence but was unsuccessful due to 200+ years of deterioration.

3i **MERCER-WILLIAMS HOUSE -** Construction of this home for Confederate Brigadier General Hugh Mercer began in 1860 but was interrupted by the Civil War. It was completed in 1868, but Mercer never occupied the home. Jim Williams, a Savannah preservationist, purchased the home in 1969. The book, Midnight in the Garden of Good and Evil, made this home a landmark. It was in the study of this home that the alleged shooting of Danny Hansford occurred. Williams was ultimately found not guilty after his fourth trial.

HSF

3j **TEMPLE MICKVE ISRAEL (c1878)**
About 5 months after Oglethorpe's original landing, a group of 42 Jews from London arrived by ship in Savannah. They immediately formed a congregation which is now considered the third oldest Jewish congregation in America. This is the only Gothic style synagogue in America.

◀ As seen in this photo from 1920, the adjacent trust lot was once occupied by First Presbyterian Church which was also a Gothic style house of worship. The church was later demolished to make way for a science building for Armstrong College.

 WALK NORTH ON BULL STREET BACK TO STOP 3.

14

FORSYTH PARK

TROLLEY STOP 4

ORIGINALLY ESTABLISHED IN THE 1840S on 10 acres of land donated by William Hodgson, the park was expanded by 20 acres and renamed in honor of Georgia Governor John Forsyth in 1851. This large park was anticipated by Oglethorpe's plan and was once the southern edge of town. Throughout its history it has served as a location for large public events and celebrations.

4a TELFAIR HOSPITAL FOR WOMEN - Now an apartment building, this building was originally built in 1884 as a women's hospital. The funding for this hospital came from Mary Telfair's will when she passed in 1875 (see 14f). When it merged in 1960 with Candler General Hospital, it had become the longest operating women's hospital in the country.

 **WALK TO THE SIDEWALK IN THE MIDDLE OF FORSYTH PARK AND WALK NORTH.**

4b CONFEDERATE MONUMENT - Erected in 1874 in honor of Confederate soldiers who died in the Civil War, this monument was made in Canada and transported to Savannah by ship so that it would never touch "Yankee" soil. A portion of Fort Sumter's flag (where the first shots of the war were fired) lies in the cornerstone. The Confederate soldier atop the monument faces toward his enemy in the North.

4c FORSYTH DUMMY FORT COMPLEX - Completed in 1915 for the Georgia National Guard, this dummy fort was used for military training during World War I. Shortly thereafter, it was abandoned and sat as an oddity in the park and in a state of disrepair for many years after that. The challenging renovation project broke ground in 2004 and the job was finally completed in February 2010. It is a fantastic place to grab lunch or a snack. There are public restrooms here as well.

4d FORSYTH FOUNTAIN - Erected in 1858, this gorgeous cast iron fountain is probably the most photographed site in Savannah. Similar fountains exist in Cuzco, Peru and Poughkeepsie, NY and all are thought to be patterned after the fountain in Paris's Place de la Concorde. The fountain has undergone extensive renovations throughout the years with the last major effort occurring in 1988.

 **CONTINUE NORTH ON THE SIDEWALK TO THE NORTHERN EDGE OF THE PARK TO 4e AND THEN WALK WEST ALONG THE EDGE OF THE PARK TO 4f.**

 **4e** **THE ARMSTRONG MANSION (C1919)** - Now serving as a law office, this grand Italian Renaissance style mansion was built for George Armstrong, a successful shipping businessman. In 1935, Armstrong's widow gave the home to the City of Savannah to serve as a junior college. Now known as Armstrong State University, it moved to the south side of town in 1966.

 WALK WEST ALONG GASTON ST. TO WHITAKER ST.

 **4f** **GEORGIA HISTORICAL SOCIETY - HODGSON HALL (c1876)** Built to house the Georgia Historical Society which was established in 1839 by the state legislature, this hall was named in memory of William Brown Hodgson, a well known scholar who was married to Margaret Telfair. The hall is open to the public and contains a wealth of historical documents and artifacts pertaining to the history of Savannah and Georgia.

 WALK BACK TO STOP 4.

MASSIE HERITAGE CENTER

$AVE $$$
Buy your tickets from
OLD TOWN TROLLEY

TROLLEY STOP 5

 In 1841, Peter Massie, a Scotsman from Glynn County, Georgia, left a $5,000 bequest to the City of Savannah "for the education of the poor children." Massie frequently passed through Savannah where he noticed many uneducated youth roaming the city's sandy streets. City authorities invested Massie's gift in stocks until a large enough sum was accumulated to build a school. The school opened in 1856 as Savannah's first free public school and it continued to operate as a school until 1974. It reopened in 1977 as a teaching museum for history and architecture, a mission that continues today. Known as "Your first stop in Georgia's first city", the museum features many interactive exhibits including a Native American Exhibit, the Heritage Classroom, Architecture Exhibit, Preservation Exhibit, and a magnificent City Plan Exhibit that is a must see.

CITY PLAN EXHIBIT ▶

 **CALHOUN SQUARE -**
Laid out in 1851, this square is named in honor of John Calhoun, a South Carolina statesman who served as the Vice President of the United States under Presidents John Quincy Adams and Andrew Jackson. There are no monuments or features in this square but it is the only square in Savannah where all of the original buildings surrounding the square are intact.

5a WESLEY MONUMENTAL UNITED METHODIST CHURCH -

This church was constructed as a monument to brothers, John and Charles Wesley, who are largely credited as founding the Methodist movement. The corner stone laying ceremony took place on August 10, 1875. However, construction proceeded slowly due to poor economic conditions at the time and a major yellow fever epidemic. The first floor was occupied in 1878 but the second level and sanctuary were not completed until 1890. The sanctuary features beautiful European stained glass with each window being dedicated to one of Methodism's historic personalities.

WALK NORTH ON ABERCORN STREET TOWARD JONES STREET

5b CLARY'S CAFE -

Made famous as a scene in John Berendt's book, *Midnight in the Garden of Good and Evil*, this café has been a favorite spot for locals since 1903. Stop in for breakfast or lunch and enjoy the eclectic atmosphere that it has become known for.

5c JONES STREET -

Considered by many to be the most elegant and beautiful street in Savannah, this street was named after Noble Jones, an original colonist who arrived with Oglethorpe on the Ann. Jones was the first colonial surveyor in the colony and he also served alongside Oglethorpe in the siege of the Spanish in St. Augustine. Walking west along Jones St. from this point provides a great opportunity to explore this luxurious area.

WALK BACK TO STOP 5

CATHEDRAL OF ST. JOHN THE BAPTIST

TROLLEY STOP 6

THE COLONIAL CHARTER OF SAVANNAH PROHIBITED CATHOLICS from settling in Savannah. The English Trustees feared that Catholics would be more loyal to the Spanish in Florida than the English. This prohibition faded shortly after the Revolutionary War and this congregation was organized around 1796. Construction began on this awe-inspiring cathedral in 1873 and was completed by the addition of the spires in 1896. It was almost totally destroyed by fire in 1898 and through diligent efforts was rebuilt by 1899. Today the Diocese of Savannah includes 90 counties in southern Georgia.

LAFAYETTE SQUARE -
Laid out in 1837, this square is named in honor of the Marquis de Lafayette, a wealthy French citizen and soldier who greatly assisted the Americans during the Revolutionary War.

◀ MARQUIS DE LAFAYETTE

6a ANDREW LOW HOUSE -
This home was built in 1849 for Andrew Low, a British cotton broker. He died in 1886, the same year that his son, William Mackay Low, married Juliette Gordon. William inherited the home from his father and the couple lived here when in Savannah. They spent most of their married life in Great Britain. Their marriage was an unhappy one and they were in the process of a divorce when William died suddenly in 1905. William left most of his substantial estate to his mistress. His American holdings including this home were left to Juliette and she lived here as a widow until her death in 1927. It was during this time that Juliette established the Girl Scouts of America.

$AVE $$$ Buy your tickets from **OLD TOWN TROLLEY**

6b GIRL SCOUT FIRST HEADQUARTERS -
Located to the rear of the Andrew Low House, this carriage house once served as the First Headquarters for the Girl Scouts. While in England in 1911, Juliette Gordon Low became acquainted with Sir Robert Baden-Powell, the founder of the Boy Scouts and Girl Guides. Juliette became particularly interested in this youth movement. She decided to return to Savannah to start an organization in America. On March 12, 1912, she gathered 18 girls and held the first meeting of the American Girl Guides, later renamed the Girl Scouts. Upon her death in 1927, Juliette willed the carriage house to the Girl Scouts of Historic Georgia. It is now open to the public as a museum.

▲ JULIETTE LOW (RIGHT) WITH TROOP 1

6c LOUISA PORTER HOME - LOCATION OF THE FIRST GIRL SCOUT MEETING -
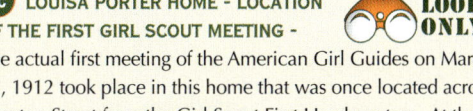 **LOOK ONLY**

The actual first meeting of the American Girl Guides on March 12, 1912 took place in this home that was once located across Drayton Street from the Girl Scout First Headquarters. At the first meeting Juliette established the first two troops known as the White Rose and Carnation patrols. Juliette's niece, Daisy Gordon, was the first registered member of the new group. The Louisa Porter Home was later demolished to make way for the office building that now occupies the lot.

▲ LOUISA PORTER HOME

6d FLANNERY O'CONNOR HOUSE -
This was the childhood home of Flannery O'Connor, an important American author with a flair for writing stories in the "Southern Gothic" style. It is known that her experiences in this home, just steps away from the Cathedral of St. John the Baptist, played a large part in her writing. Much of it reflected her Catholic faith and involved questions of morality and ethics. Unfortunately, she died from lupus at the young age of 39.

6e HAMILTON-TURNER HOUSE (c1873) -
Now a fine inn, this mansion was built for former Mayor and successful jeweler Samuel Pugh Hamilton and his wife Sarah Hamilton. It was the first home in Savannah to feature electric lights. It was also a social center for Savannah's elite in its early days. In Midnight in the Garden of Good and Evil, it was featured as the party hotspot known as Mandy's Place. Rumors persist that Mr. Hamilton and his children still make frequent surprise visits.

18

6 — WALK EAST ON CHARLTON ST. TO TROUP SQUARE

TROUP SQUARE - Laid out in 1851, this square was one of the last group of squares to be established. It was named in honor of George Michael Troup who served as a congressional representative, U.S. Senator and Governor of Georgia.

6f ARMILLARY SPHERE - Installed in the 1970's, this unique and historically controversial structure was built by Kenneth Lynch & Sons of Wilton, Connecticut. An armillary sphere is a model of the celestial globe constructed from rings which represent the equator, the tropics and other celestial circles.

6g THE CANINE FOUNTAIN - Many people believe this is the base of the Myers Drinking Fountain, a magnificent bronze structure which was originally placed in Forsyth Park in 1897 as a gift from former Mayor Herman Meyers. Unfortunately, after being removed for repairs, the original fountain was misplaced and lost. This fountain is a much smaller cast iron replica of the base of the Myers Fountain. The drinking bowls, originally set at 4 feet tall for humans, were lowered to accommodate our 4-legged friends.

6h UNITARIAN UNIVERSALIST CHURCH - JINGLE BELLS CHURCH - James L. Pierpont came to Savannah in 1853 to serve as the music director of this church. His song "One Horse Open Sleigh", later re-titled "Jingle Bells", was published in 1857. The question of where Jingle Bells was written still remains hotly contested today. Some claim that Pierpont wrote the song in 1850 while living in Medford, Massachusetts. Others claim that he wrote it while in Savannah, inspired by his younger years in New England. Either way, a reading of the original version clearly shows that it was never intended to be a Christmas song.

WALK WEST ON E. HARRIS ST. BACK TO STOP 6

7 — CITY MARKET

TROLLEY STOP 7

THIS IS A GREAT PLACE TO SHOP, TAKE IN SOME ART, DINE AND RELAX. This area was formerly a group of warehouse and shop buildings that were in close proximity to Savannah's Old City Market (see 13a). The current pedestrian areas, now closed to vehicular traffic, used to be a portion of St. Julian Street. The rehabilitation of this area began in 1985. Today's city market spreads over 4 city blocks and its buildings house many shops, restaurants and art galleries.

19

VISIT **7a** AND **7b**, THEN WALK WEST
THRU CITY MARKET TOWARD FRANKLIN SQUARE

7a **TROLLEY STOP GIFTS** - Featuring clothing, books, stationery, collectibles and souvenirs of all kinds, this large store is sure to have the perfect gift or souvenir to remember your trip to Savannah. This is also a great place to purchase discounted tickets to the attractions featured in this book.

7b **THE AMERICAN PROHIBITION MUSEUM** - In late 1917, Congress approved a proposed 18th Amendment to the US Constitution which outlawed the manufacture, sale, and transport of alcohol. The amendment was ratified by 36 of the then 48 states and became effective on January 17, 1920. Georgia lawmakers had already passed state-wide prohibition much earlier in July 1907. Many citizens did not feel they should be subject to the new law. Consequently, many speakeasies and blind tigers (illegal bars) popped up. This period also saw the rise of organized crime and murderous smuggling networks as overwhelmed police forces tried to enforce prohibition. Overall, Savannah's leadership was particularly defiant to state and national prohibition efforts and the city earned the nickname of the "Spigot of the South." Prohibition was widely viewed as an utter failure and the 18th Amendment was repealed in 1933.

This is the only museum in the country dedicated to the telling of this fascinating period of American history. It features state-of-the-art exhibits, live actors, historical memorabilia, and even an authentic operating speakeasy.

FRANKLIN SQUARE - This square was laid out in 1791, and was named in honor of Benjamin Franklin, the famous inventor and statesman. Franklin served as Georgia's colonial representative in London from 1768 to 1775.

◀ This photo from 1890 shows why this square used to be known as Water Tower Square. This masonry tower rose 80 feet above the square and served as a reservoir for the early waterworks of the city. The large steeple of the First African Baptist Church that was lost in the storm of 1893 is also visible in this photo.

7c **HAITIAN MONUMENT - (ERECTED 2007)**
This monument honors a group of around 700 free men of color from the Island of Haiti who fought beside the Americans and French in the Siege of Savannah in 1779. This group was the largest unit of men of African descent to fight in the American Revolution.

7d **FIRST AFRICAN BAPTIST (C1859)** - This church is the home of the oldest continuing black congregation in America. Andrew Bryan, a former slave who had purchased his freedom, led the church to official recognition in 1788. This facility was constructed in the 1850s by free African-Americans and slaves who were allowed to work after their normal work day. It was a stop on the Underground Railroad for runaway slaves and the holes in the floorboards of the sanctuary served as air holes for those hiding underneath.

 RETURN TO STOP 7

20

COLUMBIA SQUARE

TROLLEY STOP 8

THIS SQUARE WAS LAID OUT IN 1799 and was named after Columbia, the goddess-like national personification of the United States. The fountain located in the center of the square was donated to the city by a direct descendant of Noble Jones, an original settler who arrived with Oglethorpe on the Ann. The fountain was relocated from Noble Jones' estate, known as Wormsloe, and placed in the square in late 1971. The Wormsloe Historic Site is located on Isle of Hope near Savannah and is well worth the drive to visit and explore.

8a KEHOE HOUSE - (c1892)
William Kehoe was a poor Irish immigrant who worked his way up from being an apprentice in an iron foundry to becoming one of Savannah's most successful businessmen. This building was originally constructed as a residence for Mr. and Mrs. Kehoe and his 10 children. The Kehoe heirs sold the home in 1930 and it has since been a boarding house and a funeral parlor. It is now a fine inn. The Kehoe Iron Works Foundry building is located a few blocks to the east of this location.

8b DAVENPORT HOUSE MUSEUM - (c1820)
This Federal-style home was built by master-builder Isaiah Davenport as his family residence and a showplace of his fine

craftsmanship. By the early 20th century, the home had become a tenement house with as many as 13 families. It was slated to be demolished in 1955 to make room for a parking lot. However, a group of seven determined and civic-minded ladies formed Historic Savannah Foundation which purchased the home for $22,500 and saved it from destruction.

 NO TOUR OF SAVANNAH IS COMPLETE WITHOUT VISITING WHERE THE CITY'S PRESERVATION STORY BEGAN, THE ISAIAH DAVENPORT HOUSE.

8c KENNEDY PHARMACY - (c1890) Located at the southwest corner of Broughton and Habersham streets (to the rear of the Davenport House Museum), this building was originally built as the Anti-Migraine Pharmacy. It changed owners and names over the years and though primarily used as a pharmacy, it was also at one time a laundry and a tax office. The property was anonymously donated to HSF in 1999 for the purpose of supporting the Davenport House. In 2007, Historic Savannah Foundation, SCAD, and Davenport House Endowment Directors partnered to rehabilitate the building. The first floor is now utilized as rental and meeting space and the second floor contains a fully renovated apartment which creates income to support the operations of the Davenport House.

WALK TO SOUTH END OF COLUMBIA SQUARE AND THEN EAST ON YORK ST.

8d WEBB MILITARY MUSEUM - Opened in late 2015, this unique museum features military artifacts from the Civil War to the present which are displayed in a well laid out walk-through setting. You are invited to relive military history as you learn the stories of those who wore the uniforms, hats and medals.

WALK TO MIDDLE OF COLUMBIA SQUARE AND THEN WEST ON PRESIDENT ST.

OGLETHORPE SQUARE - This square was laid out in 1742 and was originally known as Upper New Square. It was later renamed in honor of James Edward Oglethorpe, the founder of Georgia.

8e OWENS-THOMAS HOUSE - (c1819) This English Regency style home was originally built for Richard Richardson, a cotton broker, who lost the home due to financial problems only 3 years after it was completed. It was the first of many prominent homes to be designed by architect William Jay who was 24 years old at the time. George Owens purchased the home in 1830 and it remained in his family until his granddaughter, Margaret Thomas, willed it to the Telfair Museum of Art in 1951. The Marquis de Lafayette, a wealthy French citizen and soldier who greatly assisted the Americans during the Revolutionary War, visited Savannah in 1825 to dedicate the Nathanael Greene Monument (see 11d). He stayed at this house during his visit and addressed the people of Savannah from the intricate cast iron balcony facing President Street.

WALK SOUTH ON ABERCORN ST. AND CROSS OVER OGLETHORPE AVE.

22

OLD TOWN TROLLEY TOURS 8

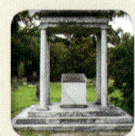

8f **COLONIAL PARK CEMETERY -** Also known as "The Old Cemetery" and "The Brick Cemetery," it was established around 1750 and was closed to further burials in 1853. Even though there are only about 600 burial markers there, it is estimated that there could be as many as 9,000 people buried here. During the Union occupation of Savannah in the Civil War, Union troops camped and stabled horses here. Many graves were desecrated during this time as some of the troops looted graves and vaults seeking valuables. They also changed the dates on some of the tombstones in a poor attempt at humor. Many of the damaged tombstones have been cemented to the cemetery's eastern wall.

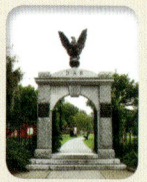

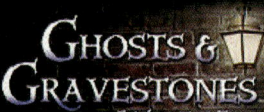

BUTTON GWINNETT MEMORIAL - A true Revolutionary hero and one of the three Georgian signers of the Declaration of Independence, Button Gwinnett is probably the most notable person buried here. Born in England around 1735, he came to Savannah in 1765 and established himself as a general trader. His enthusiasm for colonial rights and a friendship with Dr. Lyman Hall, another Georgian signer, led to his selection as a GA representative to the Continental Congress. He died from a serious leg wound that he sustained in a duel of pistols at 12 paces with his political rival, General Lachlan McIntosh, another hero of American Independence. McIntosh is also buried in this cemetery.

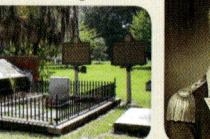

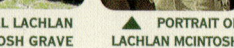

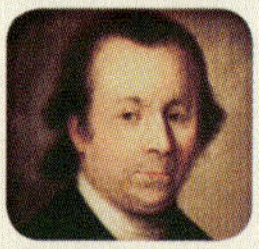

PORTRAIT OF BUTTON GWINNETT

GENERAL LACHLAN MCINTOSH GRAVE

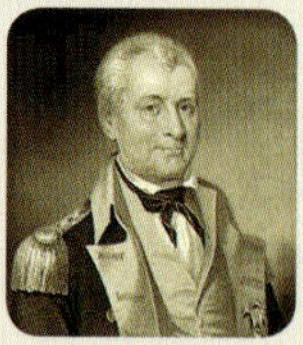

PORTRAIT OF LACHLAN MCINTOSH

WALK EAST ON OGLETHORPE AVE. TO HABERSHAM ST. TURN LEFT AND WALK NORTH ON HABERSHAM ST. BACK TO STOP 8.

GHOSTS & GRAVESTONES
Frightseeing Tour

OLD TOWN TROLLEY'S GHOSTS & GRAVESTONES - Are you interested in exploring Savannah's DARKER SIDE? Board the TROLLEY OF THE DOOMED and hear all things shadowy and sinister: The city's MYSTERIOUS HISTORY, its GRAVEST MOMENTS, its GHASTLY FOLK – it's ALL TRUE!

If you are already a passenger on an Old Town Trolley, you qualify for special discounted tickets to the Ghosts & Gravestones. Just ask an Old Town Trolley representative for more information. Space is limited and reservations are required so DON'T DELAY! Boarding for Ghosts & Gravestones occurs at Simply Savannah Gift Shop (see 10a).

OLD TOWN TROLLEY TOURS 9

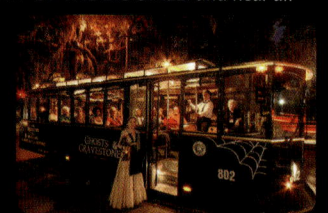

THE PIRATES' HOUSE

TROLLEY STOP 9

NOW A FAVORITE RESTAURANT, THIS BUILDING WAS ORIGINALLY A SEAMAN'S TAVERN IN THE DAYS OF SAILING SHIPS AND PIRATES. It is rumored that an underground tunnel connected the rum cellar to the river where drunken men were placed aboard ships to later awake at sea as unwitting crew members. Robert Louis Stevenson's Treasure Island was said to be inspired by events that occurred here. Captain Flint, the infamous blue-faced pirate from the book, supposedly died here in an upstairs room and is rumored to haunt the place on moonless nights.

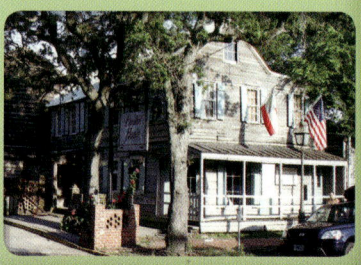

TRUSTEES' GARDEN - The area around and to the east of The Pirates' House (about 10 acres) was set aside by the Trustees in 1733 and served as an experimental farm where different crops were tested for their potential in the new colony. Some of the crops included peaches, rice, cotton, grapes, flax, hemp, indigo, olives, and mulberry trees for silk production. One of the early promises to England was that the colony of Georgia would be a significant source of silk, a sought after commodity at the time. However, silk was not a successful crop in Georgia and the garden was closed and subdivided in 1755.

9a THE HERB HOUSE (c1734) - Located right in front of the trolley stop, this home is considered the oldest surviving home in Georgia. It originally served as a home for the gardener of Trustees' Garden. When the garden failed, the Herb House was expanded into a seaman's tavern which later became The Pirates' House.

 **WALK NORTH ON E. BROAD ST. TO THE INTERSECTION WITH BAY ST.**

9b FORT WAYNE - This fort, originally known as Fort Savannah, was constructed in 1762 on the site of Trustees' Garden. Some of the original brick walls of the fort can be seen from General McIntosh Blvd. (the extension of Bay Street past East Broad Street). During the Revolutionary War, the poorly prepared Americans used this fort to defend against the British attack in 1778. The British prevailed and held Savannah as a base of operations in the south for the remainder of the war. After the war ended, the fort was renamed in honor of General "Mad Anthony" Wayne, a battle hardened American general. Wayne led the final "mop up" of the British in the south after the back-breaking American victory at Yorktown.

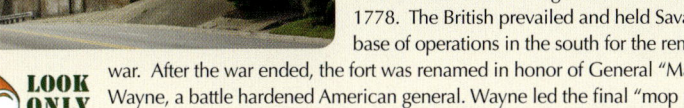

▲ GENERAL "MAD ANTHONY" WAYNE

LOOK ONLY

 **WALK WEST ON BAY ST. CROSSING OVER E. BROAD ST. CONTINUE WEST ON BAY ST. TO HOUSTON ST. TURN RIGHT AND USE CROSSWALK TO CROSS BAY ST. ONCE ACROSS BAY ST. WALK TO THE RIGHT.**

9c OLD HARBOR LIGHT (c1858) - This beacon light was constructed by the U.S. Government to guide ships past the hulls of sunken ships in the channel. The British sunk these ships in 1779 in an attempt to prevent the French navy (allies of the Americans in the Revolutionary War) from entering Savannah. The large anchors displayed around the light are remnants of historic ships that have been discovered over the years by dredging activity in the Savannah River shipping channel.

RIVER STREET RAMP - The ramp down to River Street near this location is a good chance to observe the ballast stones that were used to pave the early streets and form retaining walls along the sandy bluff. These stones were used as ballast in sailing ships which was left in Savannah after taking on a load of cotton or other exports. ▶

EMMET PARK - This park is named for the Irish Patriot Robert Emmet who was hanged by the British after leading an uprising in Dublin that was intended to gain Irish independence. As you pass through Emmet Park, you will pass by the following monuments: GA Medical Society Monument to Dr. Noble Wimberly Jones, Chatham Artillery Monument, Vietnam Memorial, the Celtic Cross, US Marine Corp Reserve Monument, the Salzburger Monument, and the Georgia Hussars Marker.

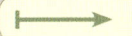 **TURN AROUND AND WALK WEST ALONG BAY STREET.**

9d CELTIC CROSS MONUMENT - Emmet Park is a special place for those of Irish descent and the Celtic Cross Ceremony is held here each year on the Sunday prior to St. Patrick's Day.

RETURN TO STOP 9

24

HISTORIC RIVER STREET

TROLLEY STOP 10

IN 1973, THE CITY BEGAN A VISIONARY PROJECT TO convert River Street from a ramshackle collection of rotten shipping wharfs into the pedestrian friendly area that you are experiencing today. It is thought to be the finest reclamation and restoration of a true antebellum shipping port in the United States. Rousakis Plaza is the formal name of most of the bricked area along the riverfront. It was named in honor of Mayor John Rousakis who served as Savannah's mayor for 21 years beginning in 1970.

10a SIMPLY SAVANNAH GIFT SHOP - If you are seeking the perfect gift for loved ones back home or a significant memento to remember your trip to Savannah, then this is your place. This shop specializes in anything and everything related to Savannah and Georgia.

10b THE ECHO CHAMBER - Directly across River Street from the Simply Savannah Gift Shop, you will find a curious spot known as the Echo Chamber. Most Savannahians don't even know about this little secret. X marks the spot where you should stand and make a little noise. A yell or a whisper is equally effective but be careful how silly you act because only the person on the X can hear the mysterious echoes.

 WALK EAST ON RIVER STREET

10c THE WAVING GIRL STATUE (ERECTED 1972) - Florence Martus (1868-1943) became known as "The Waving Girl" by sailors around the world. She spent most of her life on Elba Island (this island can be seen by walking further east on River Street and looking for the large natural gas tanks that are downriver). From the porch of her home on Elba Island, she waved a handkerchief by day and a lantern by night at ships entering or leaving the port of Savannah. It is said that she never missed waving at a single ship between 1887 and 1931 when she moved into town.

▲ This photo from 1892 shows what one would have seen along the river banks during this period. At that time, Savannah was one of the leading Naval Stores markets in the world. Naval Stores, the generic term for products derived from pine trees such as turpentine, pitch and rosin used in wooden ship construction, shared the acres of docks and storage yards alongside cotton.

◄ **FLORENCE MARTUS, THE WAVING GIRL (PHOTO C1933)**

10d OLYMPIC YACHTING CAULDRON - This cauldron was lit by the Olympic Flame from Mt. Olympus at the Savannah Opening Ceremony on July 20, 1996. The six sails represent the Olympic yachting events that were held off the coast of Savannah during the 1996 Olympic Games.

 TURN AROUND AND WALK BACK WEST ON RIVER STREET

10e THE SAVANNAH COTTON EXCHANGE (c1887) - Viewed from River Street, one can appreciate the concept of "air rights" that was utilized in the construction of this building.

10f SAVANNAH RIVERBOAT CRUISES - In 1991, Captain Jonathan Claughton accepted a brave, new challenge: bringing a dinner cruise tour to Savannah. After conducting careful research, he invested in the River Queen, a 400 passenger vessel. The company has since expanded and added two larger vessels to the fleet including the 600 passenger Savannah River Queen. The company offers a wide variety of cruises to include sightseeing, lunch and dinner cruises, murder mystery and haunted cruises, among others. Seeing Savannah from the river offers a unique perspective on the city and you will enjoy cruising with a customer service oriented company like Savannah Riverboat Cruises.

10g SAVANNAH BELLES FERRIES - This free water ferry service will take you for a ride across the Savannah River. It stops at Hutchinson Island and then the Marriott Riverfront before returning to this landing.

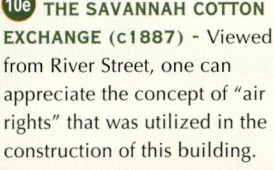

Today, Hutchinson Island, a part of Georgia, is home to the Savannah International Trade & Convention Center and the Westin Savannah Harbour Resort & Spa. This area of the island was once the site of the large Seaboard Air Line deep sea terminal where many people were employed. Prior to the existence of the original Talmadge Bridge, ferries were the only way to get to the island. Around the clock ferry service began in 1898 and ended when the bridge opened in 1954.

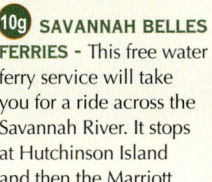

10h THE AFRICAN AMERICAN MONUMENT (ERECTED 2002) - This bronze monument features an African American family embracing with broken shackles on their feet. The monument commemorates and honors the contributions of African Americans to the cultural, social, educational, economic, and spiritual life of Savannah. The monument's inscription was written by Maya Angelou.

10i VISITORS INFORMATION CENTER - This point offers tourist information, public restrooms, and an elevator up to Bay Street.

10j WORLD WAR II MEMORIAL - Dedicated on November 7, 2010 and entitled "A World Apart", this fine monument honors living and deceased World War II veterans from Savannah and Chatham County. The 12 ton copper and bronze sphere is split to represent the Pacific and European theaters of the war. The plaques inside the spheres contain the names of the men and women from Chatham County who lost their lives in the war.

RETURN TO STOP 10

26

PARISH HOUSE / BAY STREET

 TROLLEY STOP 11

ORIGINALLY KNOWN AS THE STRAND, Bay street has been a busy thoroughfare from Savannah's earliest days based on its strategic location on top of the bluff between the river and town. Trucking which serves industries to the east of downtown and heavy commuting traffic creates significant congestion on Bay Street at certain times of the day. Various possibilities to alleviate this congestion have been explored and considered over the years but no viable alternatives have yet emerged.

 WALK SOUTH TO REYNOLDS SQUARE

REYNOLDS SQUARE - This square was laid out in 1734 and was originally named Lower New Square. It was later renamed in honor of Georgia's first Royal Governor, Sir John Reynolds.

11a JOHN WESLEY MONUMENT - (ERECTED 1969) This bronze statue of the founder of the Methodist Movement features a young John Wesley in Church of England vestments extending his right hand in love, exhortation and invitation while holding the Bible in his left. Wesley and his brother Charles arrived in Savannah in 1736 after Oglethorpe had requested that he serve as the minister of Christ Church. He is credited with starting the first protestant Sunday School and compiling the first hymnal used in Georgia. However, Wesley had a rough time while in the colony. He angered Oglethorpe and the trustees by preaching to the Indians and he also became enamored with a young lady that ended up marrying another man. After he refused to give her communion, her husband sued Wesley for defamation of character. After only a year and nine months in the colony, he quietly left town and returned to England.

11b THE FILATURE - Now occupied by a law firm, this trust lot is the former site of the Filature. This large barn like structure was erected in 1751 for the purpose of reeling and weaving silk, a commodity that was intended to be exported to England. When the silk industry failed, the building was converted to an assembly and dance hall. It served as the city's primary government building until 1812 when the government offices were moved to the City Exchange (see **12f**). During his visit of 1791, President George Washington attended a grand ball held here in his honor.

11c THE OLDE PINK HOUSE - (c1789) Now a popular restaurant, it was originally built as the residence of James Habersham, Jr. who is rumored to haunt the place. It takes its name from the pink stucco that covers its antique bricks. It avoided the great fire of 1796 and during its long history it has served as a bank, a tea room and the headquarters of one of Sherman's generals.

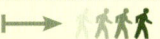 **WALK WEST ON E. ST. JULIAN ST. (TO LEFT OF OLDE PINK HOUSE). CAREFULLY CROSS DRAYTON ST. AND CONTINUE WEST TO JOHNSON SQUARE.**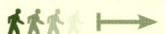

JOHNSON SQUARE - This square was the first square laid out by Oglethorpe and was named in honor of Governor Robert Johnson of South Carolina, a friend of Oglethorpe's who provided assistance and supplies to Savannah in its earliest days. This square has historically been a center of commercial and civic activities. In the early years, the lots surrounding this square contained the public store in addition to the public grist mill and oven where the colonists obtained their bread. The Declaration of Independence was publicly read in this square on August 10, 1776 and was celebrated riotously.

11d NATHANAEL GREENE MONUMENT (COMPLETED 1830) - This 50 foot marble monument, intended to resemble a Roman sword, is the grave of Nathanael Greene (and his son, George Washington Greene). A personal friend of President George Washington, Greene served as the leader of the American forces in the South during the Revolutionary War. His list of battles is too long to list here but his leadership was instrumental in defeating the British.

◀ **PORTRAIT OF NATHANAEL GREENE**

11e CHRIST CHURCH - Founded in 1733 this church is considered the "Mother Church of Georgia." This trust lot was designated by Oglethorpe as the site of the colony's house of worship but no building was erected for some time. The current structure was erected in 1838. The two most famous rectors of Christ Church, John Wesley and George Whitefield, exercised their ministry out of the colony's courthouse building which was located to the rear of the US Custom House **12d**. John Wesley (1736-1737) started the first Sunday School in America there. George Whitefield (1738-1740) is considered one of the greatest evangelists of all time and one of the men responsible for the "Great Awakening."

11f JOHNSON SQUARE BUSINESS CENTER (c1911) - Originally the Savannah Bank and Trust Building, this "skyscraper" avoided the fate of many of the other Johnson Square skyscrapers erected near the turn of the century.

◀ This is a drawing of the previous Christ Church building that was torn down to make way for the current structure. It was in this church building that President George Washington attended service while visiting Savannah during his southern tour of 1791.

11g **REGIONS BANK BUILDING -** This building was originally built as a Morrison's cafeteria but is now occupied by a bank and offices. It was previously the site of The Pulaski House hotel. Rumor has it that a young girl in period dress named Gracie Watson is occasionally seen in the basement of this building.

◀ GRACIE WATSON'S GRAVE IN BONAVENTURE CEMETERY.

◀ **THE PULASKI HOUSE HOTEL -** The age of the Pulaski House is unknown but it may date from as early as 1795. The hotel manager in 1864 was most eager to have General Sherman and some of his men stay here when they arrived in Savannah as a conquering army but Sherman let him know that "we are not in the habit of paying board." The manager of the hotel in the 1880's was W.J. Watson. His only daughter, Gracie Watson, died of pneumonia in 1889 at the age of six. Her marker featuring a detailed sculpture of Gracie is the most visited grave in Bonaventure Cemetery.

11h **SUNTRUST BANK BUILDING -** This office building and its associated parking deck took the place of three elaborate "skyscrapers" that were demolished in 1975 to make way for this project.

11i **SUNTRUST BANK BUILDING PARKING DECK -** This corner was previously occupied by the dramatic Liberty Bank and Trust building.

▲ Photo of the Liberty Bank and Trust building that was lost in 1975.

▲ This is a view north toward Johnson Square from Bull and Broughton Streets in the late 1800's.

▲ Broughton Street was the primary business district of Savannah from the 1920's through 1950's. Can you identify where today's Panera Bread is located?

TURN LEFT ON BROUGHTON ST. AND WALK EAST BACK TO ABERCORN ST. TURN LEFT AND WALK NORTH THRU REYNOLDS SQUARE BACK TO STOP 11.

EXCHANGE BELL - FACTOR'S WALK

TROLLEY STOP 12

CITY EXCHANGE FIRE BELL - This is a small replica of the City Exchange bell tower. The fire bell hanging in this replica tower was imported from Amsterdam and dates from 1802. It originally hung in the City Exchange tower which was manned every night due to the ever present threat of fires (See 12f).

 WALK WEST ALONG BAY ST. FOR TOUR 12.

12a FACTOR'S ROW AND FACTOR'S WALK - This collection of buildings that appear to be two to three stories tall from Bay Street are really five to six story buildings that have their first floors on River Street. Now occupied with a mix of retail stores, restaurants, offices and residential units, these buildings used to be the Wall Street of Savannah when cotton was king. Named for the cotton factors or brokers, the upper levels of these buildings served as offices. The lower levels served as warehouses for cotton and naval stores that were loaded and unloaded from ships docked along River Street. From the bridges and walkways over Factor's Walk, one can see the ballast stones that were used to pave streets and build retaining walls on the sandy bluff. These ballast stones were used as ballast in sailing ships which was left in Savannah after taking on a load of cotton or other exports.

This photo (c1867) shows some of the Factor's Row buildings with a busy river in the background.

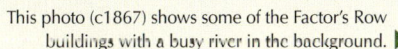

Sampling Cotton in the 1890's on River Street

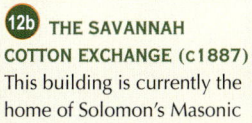

12b THE SAVANNAH COTTON EXCHANGE (C1887) This building is currently the home of Solomon's Masonic Lodge Number One. It was originally constructed to house the Cotton Exchange to further the interests of cotton merchants. At the time, Savannah and Liverpool, England were the only two places in the world where the price of cotton was quoted. It was the first building in America to incorporate "air rights" as it was constructed over the Drayton Street ramp that descends to the river. This fact can be seen more readily from River Street. The original terra cotta griffon fountain (c 1889-seen in photo) in front of the Exchange was destroyed by a spectacular single car crash in 2008. It was painstakingly reconstructed over 10 months to form a mold for the new concrete replica that was rededicated in December 2009. A griffon is a mythological beast that served to guard ancient treasure. The griffon fountain is surrounded by elaborate ironwork featuring profiles of famous statesmen and poets. This ironwork was originally located at the Barclay-Wetter House.

$AVE $$$
Buy your tickets from
OLD TOWN TROLLEY

12c COOL SAVANNAH TOURS & GIFTS - Step inside a historic former cotton factor's office and shop for historic memorabilia and unique souvenirs. This location is also the starting point for multiple professionally guided walking tours including historic tours, spooky ghost tours and the haunted pub tour. Old Town Trolley sells discounted tickets to all of these fantastic tours.

12d US CUSTOM HOUSE (c1852) - The granite used in the construction of this substantial all stone building was shipped from a quarry in Quincy, Massachusetts. It is notable for its six monolithic columns which weigh 15 tons apiece. A plaque recognizes that this building occupies the site of Oglethorpe's former wood frame residence and headquarters. It was also the site of the city's first public building which stood on the rear of the lot where John Wesley preached one of his first sermons in America in 1736.

From your vantage point at Washington's Guns, look ahead to the west at the intersection of Bay and Bull Streets. This sketch shows General Sherman's Union Army entering Savannah on December 21, 1864. ▶

12e WASHINGTON'S GUNS - These guns known locally as "George and Martha" were captured from the British at the Battle of Yorktown. They were presented to the Chatham Artillery by President George Washington during his visit into Savannah in 1791 in appreciation of their service.

◀ Sherman's massive force of 62,000 men was able to take Savannah without a fight because the Confederate Army, about 10,000 men, had used pontoon bridges to retreat into South Carolina during the night of December 20, 1864. This decision to retreat saved Savannah from certain destruction.

12f CITY HALL (c1905) - The interior of this public building features an impressive rotunda 30 feet wide and rising 70 feet high to a beautiful stained glass dome. The exterior of the dome is gilded with a thin layer of 23kt gold. City Hall occupies the former site of the City Exchange.

CITY EXCHANGE (c1799) - This building served both public and private interests until it was acquired by the city in 1812. It was demolished in 1904 to make way for City Hall. A small replica of the City Exchange tower and its fire bell can be seen a few hundred feet east on Bay Street. ▶

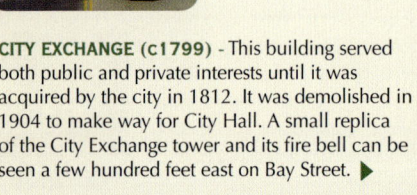

▲ This photo shows what a view down Bull Street from the City Exchange bell tower in 1890 would have looked like. Note the ability to see the squares and monuments clearly down Bull Street.

12g HISTORIC SAVANNAH CARRIAGE TOURS - Touring Savannah by horse-drawn carriage is a wonderful way to see the city. Tour guides will inform and entertain as you relax in a comfortable carriage pulled by beautiful horses. From smaller romantic carriages to larger group carriages, Historic Savannah Carriage Tours offers a wide range of enjoyable tours.

12h OGLETHORPE'S BENCH - This location is arguably where the recorded history of Savannah started. Erected in 1906, this granite bench marks the approximate location of Oglethorpe's tent where he spent his first night in Georgia while scouting out potential sites for the colony. It also marks the landing site of the first colonists which took place about a week after Oglethorpe's original scouting visit. Keep in mind that River Street did not exist at that time and this area was the top of a high sandy bluff.

This photo shows Oglethorpe's Bench and the surrounding buildings in 1909. ▼

RETURN TO STOP 12

ELLIS SQUARE - SAVANNAH'S NEWEST OLD SQUARE

TROLLEY STOP 13

THIS SQUARE WAS ONE OF THE ORIGINAL FOUR LAID OUT IN 1733.

It was named Ellis Square in honor of Henry Ellis, the second Royal Governor of Georgia. In 1763, the colonial legislature moved the public market from Wright Square to Ellis Square. This square has been commonly known as Market Square ever since.

WALK SOUTH THRU ELLIS SQUARE AND THEN EAST ON W. CONGRESS ST.

13a OLD CITY MARKET -
Numerous market structures were built in Ellis Square over the years but the "Old City Market" building was completed in 1872. It served as a market until 1950 when it was demolished to make way for a parking deck. The loss of this treasure was one of the last straws which led to organized historic preservation efforts in Savannah. The city ultimately reclaimed the site and opened a new interactive Ellis Square in 2010.

13b PAULA DEEN'S THE LADY AND SONS RESTAURANT -
In 1989 Paula Deen started a lunch delivery service called "The Bag Lady" out of her home. The business grew and eventually became a full service restaurant known as "The Lady" which was located in the Best Western hotel on the Southside of town. The restaurant moved downtown in 1996 and was renamed "The Lady & Sons." It moved once more to its current location which opened in November 2003. If you are hungry for delicious southern home cooking, this is the place.

THE PAULA DEEN TOUR
Ask an Old Town Trolley Representative how you can join in on The Paula Deen Tour. Hear the complete story of her rags to riches rise to stardom and all the most up to date Paula Deen "DISH"!

TURN RIGHT ON WHITAKER ST. AND WALK SOUTH TO BROUGHTON ST. TURN RIGHT AND WALK WEST ON BROUGHTON ST.

13c TONDEE'S LONG ROOM -
Built in 1767 at the Northwest corner of Broughton Street and Whitaker, this tavern served as a meeting place for a group of young men seeking American independence who became known as the "Liberty Boys." On June 4, 1775, instead of celebrating King George III's birthday as was tradition, the Liberty Boys raised a liberty pole to celebrate the birth of liberty. The tavern continued to serve as an important meeting place for revolutionary activities until the British occupation of Savannah in 1778. The revolutionary government of Georgia reconvened at the tavern after the war's end in 1782. Unfortunately, this birthplace of liberty in Georgia burned in the Great Fire of 1796.

RAISING THE LIBERTY POLE ▶

CONTINUE WALKING WEST ON BROUGHTON STREET TO BARNARD STREET. TURN LEFT AND WALK SOUTH ON BARNARD STREET TO TELFAIR SQUARE.

TELFAIR SQUARE -
One of the first 4 squares laid out in 1733, this square was originally named St. James' Square in honor of the royal residence in London. In early days, it was one of the most fashionable neighborhoods in Savannah. It was also the site of The Government House which served as the residence of the Royal Governors of Georgia. The square was renamed in 1883 to honor the philanthropic Telfair family.

◀ From Telfair Square between 1872 and 1950, one would have seen the Old City Market 13a by looking north on Barnard Street.

13d FIRST CHATHAM BANK BUILDING -
This building occupies the former location of the home of George Walton, a signer of the Declaration of Independence.

◀ This site was later the location of the Odd Fellows' Hall (photo c1888).

◀ This is a photo of the home of George Walton (built between 1784 and 1790). This is where President George Washington stayed while in Savannah during his southern tour of 1791.

13e TELFAIR ACADEMY OF ARTS AND SCIENCES -
Built on the original site of The Government House (the residence of the royal governors of Georgia), this building was completed in 1819 for Alexander Telfair, the son of Governor Edward Telfair. This Regency-style mansion served as the family's home until 1875. Mary Telfair, Alexander's sister and an early patron of the arts, bequeathed the home and its furnishings to the Georgia Historical Society to be used as a museum. It is the oldest public museum in the South.

13f TRINITY UNITED METHODIST CHURCH - (C1848)
This church is the oldest Methodist Church in Georgia. The building is a Corinthian Greek Revival style and it resembles the design of Wesley Chapel in England.

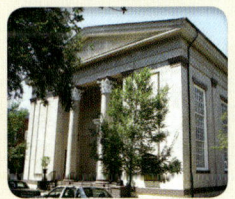

13g THE JEPSON CENTER FOR THE ARTS -
Designed by internationally renowned architect, Moshe Safdie, this museum opened in March 2006 and features 20th and 21st century art in addition to hosting traveling shows.

13h FEDERAL BUILDING COMPLEX -
The three federal government buildings fronting Telfair Square were constructed in the early 1980's and are known by most locals as the "Bathroom Tile Buildings." They were a disjointed architectural addition to one of Savannah's finest historical squares. The federal government allowed the construction of these buildings even though there was significant opposition to their design.

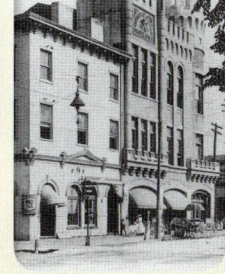

◀ This photo shows some of the unique architecture that once stood at the Southeast corner of Barnard and York streets. It is now the location of the Juliette Gordon Low Federal Building, one of the Bathroom Tile Buildings.

WALK NORTH ON BARNARD ST. TOWARD ELLIS SQUARE AND RETURN TO STOP 13.

SHIPS OF THE SEA MARITIME MUSEUM

TROLLEY STOP 14

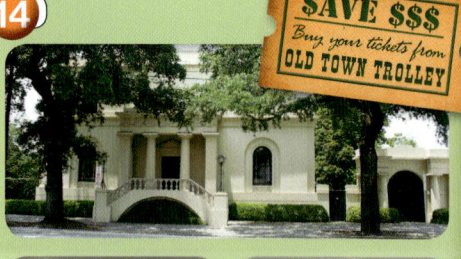

BUILT IN 1819, THIS HOME WAS DESIGNED BY WILLIAM JAY and was originally known as the Scarbrough House. It was built for William Scarbrough, a successful shipping merchant who moved to Savannah in 1802. In 1818, he became the principal investor and president of the Savannah Steamship Company. The company built the steamship, the SS Savannah, which became the first steamship to successfully cross the Atlantic in 1819. Unfortunately, the project was a money pit and it sunk the fortunes of many prominent Savannahians including Scarbrough, who lost his home and was declared insolvent in 1820. The home served as a public school from 1878 until 1962. Afterward, it sat abandoned until Historic Savannah Foundation restored the building in the 1970's. The building is now home to the Ships of the Sea Museum which opened in 1997. It features a vast display of large model ships and all things nautical. This magnificent museum demands a stop of its own and should not be missed.

▲ THE STEAMSHIP SAVANNAH

OLD TOWN TROLLEY WELCOME CENTER

TROLLEY STOP 15

LOCATED NEAR THE BASE OF THE TALMADGE BRIDGE, this is a convenient stop to purchase tickets to the attractions featured in this book. Expect to be greeted by knowledgeable and friendly Old Town Trolley team members who can assist you with planning out your visit to Savannah. Hungry? This is a great spot to hop off for a quick and tasty lunch or snack from the restaurants inside. A small convenience store is located in the building as well.

◀ Dedicated as a memorial to Eugene Talmadge, who served as the Governor of Georgia from 1933-1937 and 1941-1943, the new cable-stayed Talmadge Memorial Bridge was completed in 1991. It provides a vertical clearance of 185 feet for the ships passing below. The original Talmadge Bridge was a cantilever truss design. The completion of this bridge in 1954 led to the termination of the Hutchinson Island ferry service (see). That bridge only had a vertical clearance of 136 feet. As modern ships grew larger, this bridge suffered two ship-bridge collisions in 1983 and 1990. Some of the concrete piers of the old bridge still stand beside the new bridge.

HISTORIC TOURS OF AMERICA
The Nation's Storyteller

AMERICA'S MOST TRUSTED TOURS, ATTRACTIONS, FESTIVAL MARKETPLACES & THEMED RETAIL

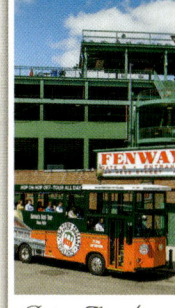
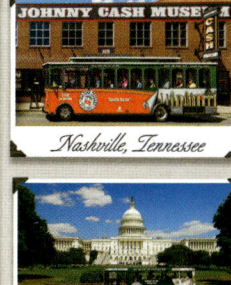

Key West, Florida   *Nashville, Tennessee*

San Diego, California   *St. Augustine, Florida*   *Boston, Massachusetts*   *Washington, D.C.*   *Savannah, Georgia*

HistoricTours.com | 800-TOUR-HTA

Historic Tours of America, Old Town Trolley Tours and Transportainment are all registered trademarks of Historic Tours of America, Inc. Ghosts & Gravestones and Frightseeing are registered service marks of Historic Tours of America®

PHOTO CREDITS

Armstrong Atlantic University, Lane Library, Florence Powell Minis Collection - Multiple Images - Artwork of Savannah, W.H. Parish Publishing co., 1893

Central of Georgia Railway Historical Society, Inc. - Point 1e - Aerial of Railroad Complex

Jacob Blumenfeld - photographer of Massie Heritage Center - City Plan Exhibit - Stop 5

Dennis McDonald - photographer of Talmadge Bridges - Stop 15 - www.worldofstock.com

Georgia Historical Society - www.georgiahistory.com – Various Historic Drawings & Photos - View of Savannah 1734 pg 5, Naval Stores pages 6, 25, Street Scene pg 9, Old City Market exterior/interior pg 33, George Walton Home pg 34, Odd Fellows' Hall pg 34, Castle Hall pg 34, Tomochichi pg 10, Old County Courthouse pg 10, 1834 Lutheran Church pg 11, Madison Square pg 12, DeSoto Billboard pg 13, Presbyterian Church & Temple Mickve pg 14, Louisa Porter Home pg 18, Florence Martus at Elba & Portrait pg 25, Sherman Entering Savannah pg 31, Pontoon Bridge pg 31, SS Savannah pg 35

COPYRIGHT 2013 BY PAUL C. BLAND, AUTHOR
ISBN 978-0-615-52401-6

DISTRIBUTED BY:
COASTAL BOOKS & SOUVENIRS, LLC
SAVANNAH, GA

PROUDLY PRINTED IN SAVANNAH, GA

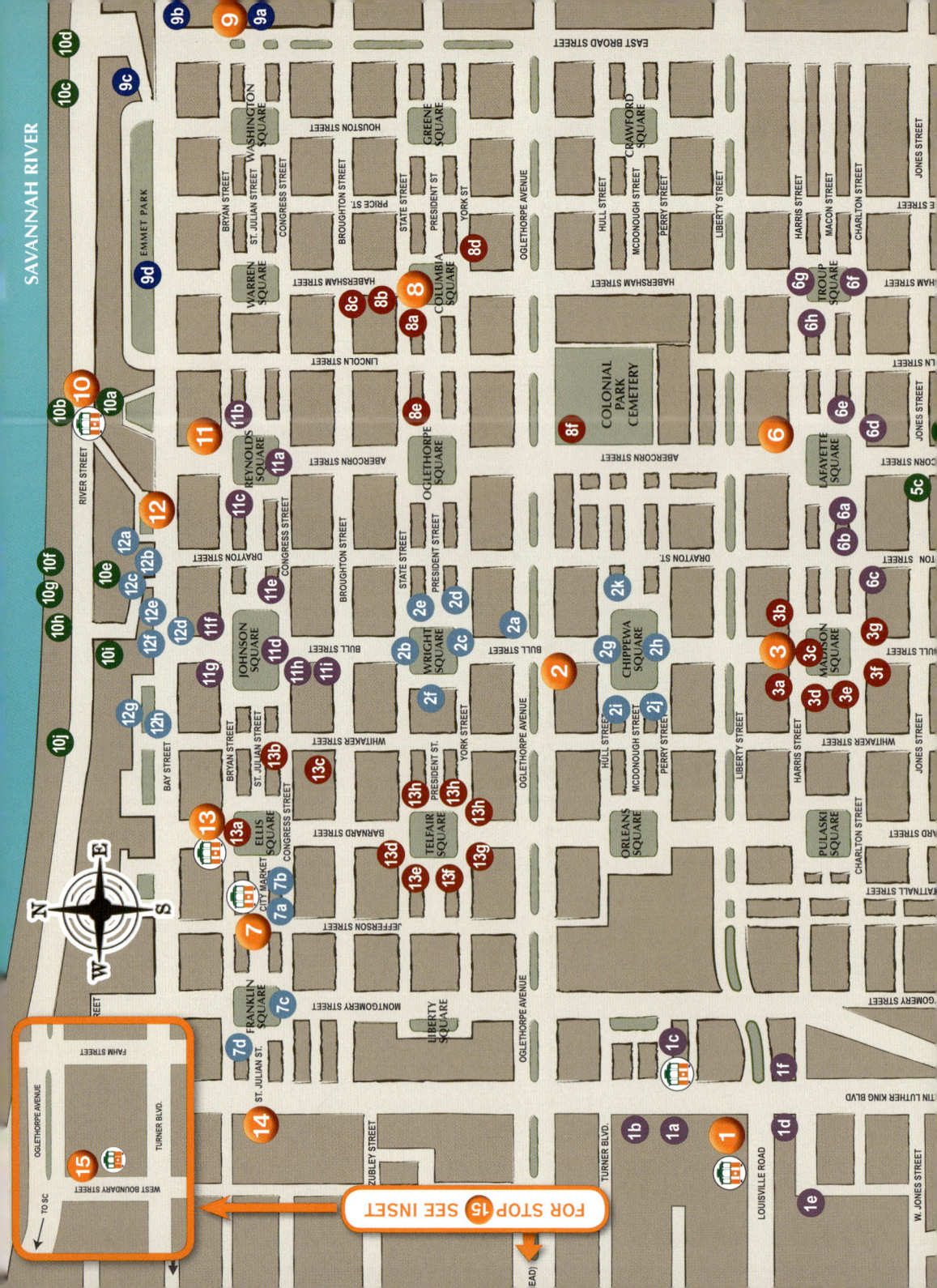